OPTICAL ILLUSIONS

INNOVATIVE DESIGNS
FOR THE MODERN QUILTER

OPTICAL ILLUSIONS
INNOVATIVE DESIGNS FOR THE MODERN QUILTER

EDITOR: Deb Rowden
DESIGNER: Sarah Meiers
PHOTOGRAPHY: Aaron T. Leimkuehler
ILLUSTRATION: Eric Sears
TECHNICAL EDITORS: Jenifer Dick, Lisa Calle
PHOTO EDITOR: Jo Ann Groves

Published by:
Kansas City Star Books
1729 Grand Blvd.
Kansas City, Missouri, USA 64108

First edition, first printing
ISBN: 978-1-61169-136-8

Kansas City Star Quilts moves quickly to publicize
corrections to our books. You can find corrections
at **www.KansasCityStarQuilts.com**, then click on
'Corrections.'

Library of Congress Control Number: **2014942810**

Printed in the United States of America by Walsworth
Publishing Co., Marceline, MO

To order copies, call StarInfo at (816) 234-4473.

CONTENTS

ACKNOWLEDGMENTS

Special thanks to the quilt holders in our photos:
Sara Kirpes, Ryan Pope, Alicia Futrelle and Abe Dick.

Most of all: to the enthusiastic participants in this quilting adventure! Modern quilting breathes wonderful new life into our quilting world.

AN INTRODUCTION TO OPTICAL ILLUSION

Optical illusions = visually perceived images that differ from reality.

Optical illusion designs can be created by:

→ Depth and motion perception.

→ Cognitive illusions — ones where your mind works to finish a perceived image.

→ The inspiration of art that explores optical illusions, such as work by M.C. Escher and Salvador Dali.

→ Op Art — the trendy style that uses optical illusions to create the impression of movement, hidden images and patterns.

→ Trompe-l'œil — a French term for tricking the eye by depicting objects in two dimensions that really exist in three dimensions (think of Wile E. Coyote painting a tunnel entrance on a rock wall for the Road Runner to smash into ...).

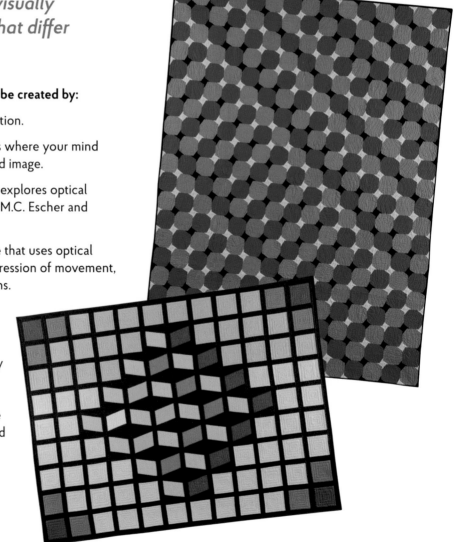

Optical illusions are not new to quilting. Quilt designs use pattern: to trick your eyes into believing they are seeing something they are not, or to cause a secondary pattern to emerge. Quilts use color — lights and darks, contrast and shading — to alter designs.

Drawing on that traditional concept, we issued a challenge to modern quilters: create a quilt with a strong optical illusion that is distinctively modern.

The response was enthusiastic. This book is the result. Here's what you'll find:

Jessica Toye's **WATER RIPPLES** (page 16) is simple to sew yet appears quite complex. Her rippling design uses only one block, one that any beginner could stitch.

BLURRED VISION (page 22) by Penny Layman likewise works with a simple design. It fools you as it seems to tip and tilt — but all you have to cut are squares.

Melissa Corry found her muse for **OLD DUTCH** (page 28) in the prairie countryside, when staring too long at simple windmills fooled her into thinking they were advancing toward her.

The repetition of triangles inspired Tia Curtis — see them racing through her **TROPICAL STORM** on page 36.

Katie Larson came up with **CURVILINEAR** (page 42), a tribute to quilters throughout history that have stitched together triangles that appear to curve.

Colors can create optical illusions too, as Jaime David proves with **AURA** (page 50). She found she could not stop at just one, making another color version of the same design — check it out on page 55.

Karen Hansen's pulsating **SURF'S UP!** (page 56) also explores the effect water's movement can have on our eye — "the blue waves rolling into shore, breaking on the sand in the sunlight ..."

The father of Op Art, Victor Vasarely, influenced Jenifer Dick's design of **3-D DIAMONDS** (page 66). Jenifer began with a traditional Tumbling block and turned it into an unexpected illusion.

Another traditional block design came into play in Mary Kay Fosnacht's **TANGERINE TUMBLER** to create her simple quilt with big impact. It's on page 72.

Enjoy these exciting designs, but don't stop there. We hope this inspires you to create your own optical illusions — see the box below for even more traditional blocks that could become optical illusions. ✕

TRADITIONAL BLOCKS THAT FORM OPTICAL ILLUSIONS

Tumbling Block (many variations)	Robbing Peter to Pay Paul
Log Cabin	Fans (including New York Beauty)
Stripes and Bars	Kaleidoscope
1,000 Pyramids	Ocean Waves
Monkey Wrench	Spiderweb
Delectable Mountains	Drunkard's Path
Hexagons	Wheel of Mystery
Double Wedding Ring	Mill Wheel
	Tessellating patterns

QUILTING ADVICE FOR OPTICAL ILLUSIONS

BY ANGELA WALTERS

"You may have heard the phrase, 'It's not a quilt until it's quilted.' That statement is just as true for quilting optical illusion quilts. But what if you aren't sure what designs to use on your quilt? There is nothing more frustrating than staring at a quilt top with no idea how to quilt it. Here are some of my favorite tips for choosing quilting designs."

But first ... a disclaimer.

Quilting is subjective. What one quilter likes, another might not. These tips are what works for me. They are simply suggestions. Use them as starting points on the road to quilting.

TIPS FOR CHOOSING QUILTING DESIGNS

1. SELECTING THREAD COLOR

Some quilts look great with bold quilting in a contrasting color, but that is probably not the best choice for an optical illusion quilt. In my opinion, the best quilting enhances a quilt without distracting from the pattern. That's why picking out the right thread color is so important. Using a thread color that blends places the emphasis on the pattern and keeps the quilting from overwhelming the quilt. It also allows you to use several different designs on the same quilt without overwhelming the quilt pattern.

Finding that perfect thread color for your quilt isn't hard at all. When I am choosing thread colors, I start by laying them across the quilt top. Since I don't have any endless supply of thread colors (as much as I wish I did!), I try to find a color that matches as closely as possible.

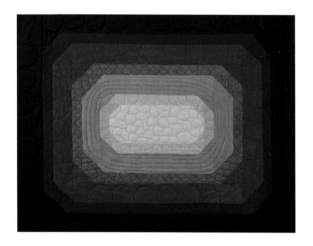

The **AURA** quilt is the perfect example of how the thread color can make a big difference. This pattern is striking due to the colors that Jaime David chose. Using a single thread color would have distracted from the pattern and the overall optical illusion.

While changing the threads probably took a little longer, the result is well worth it.

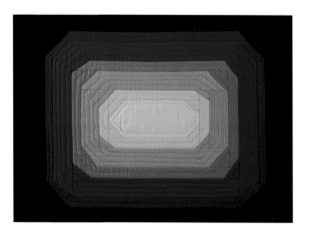

WHAT IF I HAVE TO PICK JUST ONE?

Sometimes, you won't have the option of using different colors of thread on your quilt. If you come across a quilt like that, try to find a neutral color that blends with most of the fabrics. For instance, a medium or light grey thread would be an option for a black and white quilt. I usually veer toward colors that are on the lighter side. Personally, I would rather use a lighter thread on darker fabric, then a darker thread on lighter fabric.

When quilting **OLD DUTCH**, Melissa Corry chose a stunning quilting design. Even though the quilt top was pieced with several different colored fabrics, she was able to find a thread color that allowed the quilting to shine without overwhelming the quilt.

2. GET INSPIRED BY THE PATTERN

Sometimes, you don't have to look too far for quilting inspiration. One of my all-time favorite ways to pick out quilting designs is to get inspired by the quilt itself. Using elements of the quilt pattern in the quilting can really pull the whole quilt design together.

Jenifer Dick did just that with her **3-D DIAMONDS** quilt. By echoing the square and diamond shapes in the quilting, quilter Tia Curtis shows how the right quilting designs can place all the emphasis on the quilt pattern.

3. PICK MORE THAN ONE DESIGN

Who says you have to just pick one quilting design? I think machine quilting is the funnest part of making a quilt, so I find it hard to pick just one design. (This is where matching thread color comes in handy.) Try picking out a few different quilting designs. It can add a great deal of interest to the quilt and might even make the quilting process even more fun!

The quilting on **TROPICAL STORM** is a perfect example of that. Tia Curtis used several different designs in the triangles including curved, straight and loopy lines. The effect is stunning.

4. TALK TO YOURSELF

You are the expert of your opinion. Asking yourself questions about the quilt can help you decide how to go about quilting it. More often than not, these questions will help get your creativity flowing.

So — if picking out quilting designs has you stumped, try asking yourself the following: *(Answer yourself out loud if you need to!)*

+ What is the most important thing about this quilt and how can I make the quilting enhance it?

Picking out the most important thing about the quilt forces you to verbalize your quilting priorities. If the most important thing is the quilt pattern, what designs can you pick to enhance it? Is the most important thing the fact that it is being made for a 5-year-old boy who will love it to death? Maybe some dense quilting would be the way to go. No matter the answer, this question gets you closer to choosing the perfect design.

+ Is there a desired effect I would like to achieve with the quilting?

For instance, do you want to add movement to the quilt? Do you like a lot of texture with the quilting? Do you want the quilting to contrast with or complement the quilt pattern? Once you know what effect you are going for, you can easily eliminate designs that don't work.

TANGARINE TUMBLER is a great example of using quilting to contrast with the quilt pattern. This quilt pattern is bold, graphic and all-around stunning. Mary Kay Fosnacht chose to add contrast with the quilting by using curvy, circular quilting designs.

→ Can I combine two designs to achieve a different look?

Combining two different designs is an easy way to add a different texture to your quilt. Karen Hansen combined wavy lines and pebbles in her **SURF'S UP!** quilt.

Most quilting designs can be easily combined, so try pairing up some of your favorites.

→ What quilting designs do I want to use? Do I have a favorite design that I could incorporate in the quilting?

Although that can sound like a vague question, the answer is definitely specific. Pick the quilting designs and applications that appeal to you. After all, it is your quilt. The art of quilting, from the quilt pattern to the quilting, is a creative outlet. That means it should be fun and enjoyable. Don't stress over the quilting or force yourself to use quilting designs you don't like.

4. EMBRACE THE UNEXPECTED

It's possible to think too hard about which quilting designs to use. Instead of trying to think of the "right" ones, try coming up with unexpected ways to quilt the quilt top. Since I am easily amused, this tactic never fails to put a smile on my face. Using designs in different ways, or "unexpected" designs, makes the quilting process more fun. It also seems to draw people in closer to look at the quilt.

Penny Layman hit the nail on the head with her **BLURRED VISION** quilt. Instead of going with classic quilting designs, she used fun, unexpected designs to create a completely unique texture.

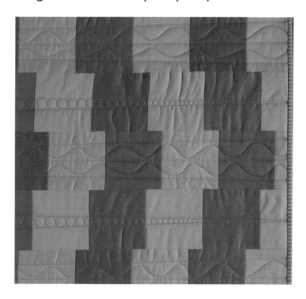

5. ABOVE ALL, REMEMBER THIS: RELAX AND HAVE FUN!

Happy Quilting! ✖

ANGELA WALTERS

Angela is a longarm quilter, teacher and the author of several books, including "Machine Quilting for the Modern Quilt" and "In the Studio with Angela Walters." Her quilting career began at the side of her husband's grandfather: together, the two made Angela's first quilt, a nine-patch that is still on her bed today. Thousands of swirls, feathers and parallel lines later, Angela has turned her love of stitches and fabric into a thriving business focused on modern machine quilting. Today, she lives on the outskirts of Kansas City with her husband Jeremy, three children, and many, many quilts. Learn more about Angela and her work at **www.quiltingismytherapy.com**.

OPTICAL ILLUSIONS

THE CREATIVITY OF
LAWRENCE, KANSAS, SPILLS
OVER INTO ITS DOWNTOWN
ALLEYS, WHERE OUR
LOCATION PHOTOGRAPHS
WERE SHOT.

WATER RIPPLES

MADE AND QUILTED BY JESSICA TOYE

60" × 80" | BLOCK: 4" × 4"

> " *I have always loved optical illusions and geometric designs in art. When I started working on this project, I wanted to make a quilt that appeared more complex than it was to construct. My goal was to design something dynamic, with lots of movement, but forgiving to assemble. Using solid fabrics helps streamline the design and reduce distractions from the design. The biggest challenge of this quilt is putting the blocks in just the right order to create the visual rippling.* "

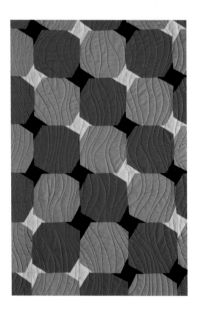

FABRIC/SUPPLIES

+ 2 ¼ yards dark turquoise solid

+ 2 ¼ yards light turquoise solid

+ 2 yards white solid

+ 2 ⅓ yards black solid for blocks and binding

+ 4 ¾ yards solid white for backing

+ Template plastic

+ White chalk pencil

CUTTING

BLOCKS

→ From the dark turquoise, cut 17 – 4 ½" × width of fabric strips. Subcut each strip into 9 – 4 ½" × 4 ½" squares (150 total).

→ From the light turquoise, cut 17 – 4 ½" × width of fabric strips. Subcut each strip into 9 – 4 ½" × 4 ½" squares (150 total).

→ From the white, cut 27 – 2 ½" × width of fabric strips. Subcut each strip into 24 – 2 ½" × 1 ¾" rectangles (make a minimum of 641).

→ From the black, cut 31 – 2 ½" × width of fabric strips.

   ▪ Set aside 7 strips for binding.

   ▪ Subcut each of the remaining 24 strips into 24 – 2 ½" × 1 ¾" rectangles (make a minimum of 559).

PIECING

Using the template plastic, make the Water Ripples template (page 19).

The quilt is made of 300 – 4" × 4" blocks. For the correct layout for each block and the number of each to make, use the Assembly Chart.

BLOCK ASSEMBLY

Place the template on the right side of each turquoise square. Use a white chalk pencil to mark around the template.

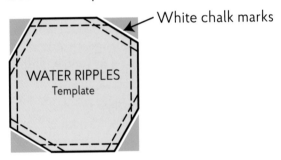

White chalk marks

WATER RIPPLES
Template

Align one long edge of a small rectangle with the chalk mark so the small rectangle is mostly on top of the turquoise, with just a bit of turquoise showing in the corner with right sides together. Try to have the rectangle overhang both edges evenly as shown. Stitch the rectangle to the square ¼" away from chalk line. Press toward the corner.

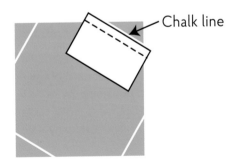

Chalk line

Repeat to sew the rectangles onto the remaining 3 corners. Trim off the excess fabric to square up the block. Use the edges of the turquoise fabric as your guide for where to trim. Make 300 – 4½" blocks.

ASSEMBLY

To assemble the quilt top, use your design wall or a large, flat surface to arrange the blocks. Follow the Assembly Diagram (page 20) — it labels the blocks and shows their rotation to assist you in laying out your quilt top.

Note: The most difficult part of making this quilt is maintaining the proper block arrangement. It is helpful to use a design wall or large flat surface to lay out the blocks and see the arrangement before the blocks are sewn together. It is easy to get blocks mixed up, so pay close attention to what you are sewing.

* Sew the blocks into rows. Press the seams to one side, alternating the direction of pressing from row to row.

* Slide the seams against each other to make sure the seams are lined up before stitching the rows together. It's helpful to use pins on both sides of the seam (in the seam allowance) to ensure they stay in place and to keep your sewing machine from flipping or bunching the seam allowances as you sew. Press.

Assembly Chart

Block A
Make 40 blocks

Block B
Make 40 blocks

Block C
Make 61 blocks

Block D
Make 60 blocks

Block E
Make 49 blocks

Block F
Make 50 blocks

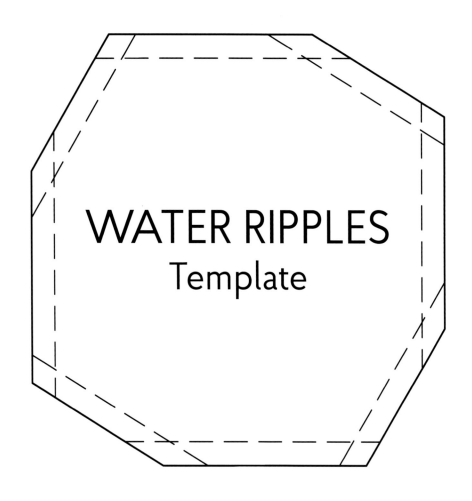

WATER RIPPLES
Template

1 inch

FINISHING

BACKING

Piece the backing into a 68" × 88" rectangle.

QUILTING

Water Ripples was quilted on a longarm machine using a curvy line stretching across the length of the quilt. This design was chosen to reinforce the rippling illusion created by the arrangement of blocks.

BINDING

Join the 7 – 2½" black strips to make about 280" of binding. Bind. ⚼

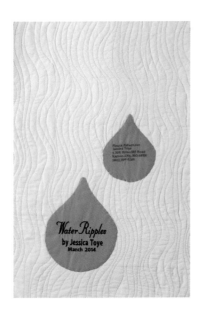

Assembly Diagram

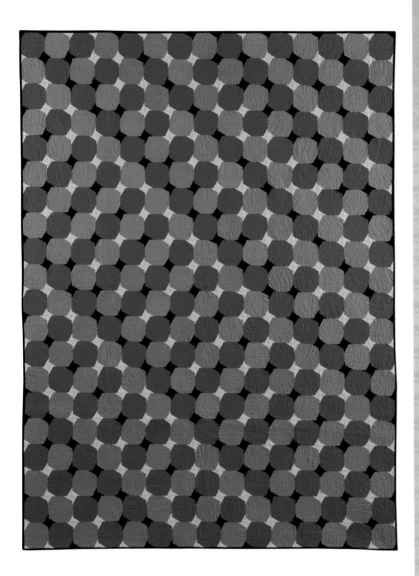

JESSICA TOYE

Jessica Toye lives in Kansas City, Missouri, with her husband, Jason, and adorable son, Daniel. Jessica learned to sew at a very early age from her mother and has been quilting since about 2003. She is an active member of the Kansas City Modern Quilt Guild and a professional longarm quilter. You can find her online at **JessToyeQuilts.wordpress.com**.

Thanks to my family of design critics and fabric selection assistants for their support, encouragement and inspiration.

BLURRED VISION

MADE BY PENNY LAYMAN | QUILTED BY SUSAN SANTISTEVAN
64" × 80"

> " *For this design, I searched online for optical illusions. This type of illusion grabbed my attention because of its simplicity, boldness and effectiveness. Although all the rows are the same width from one edge to the other, they appear to be smaller on one edge and larger on the other edge.* "

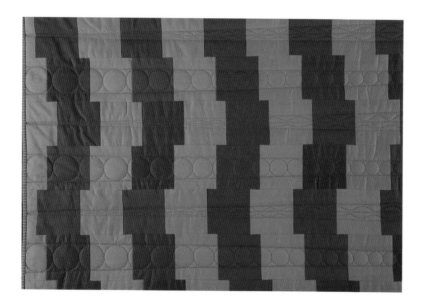

FABRIC/ SUPPLIES

- 3 yards green
- 3 ⅔ yards blue for top and binding
- 4 yards for backing

CUTTING

- From the green, cut 160 – 4½" × 4½" squares.
- From the blue, cut:
    1. 140 – 4½" × 4½" squares
    1. 10 – 1½" × 4½" rectangles
    1. 20 – 2½" × 4½" rectangles
    1. 10 – 4½" × 4½" rectangles

BINDING

- From the blue, cut 8 strips 2½" × width of fabric.

PIECING

Sew together alternating squares of 7 blue and 8 green, beginning
and ending with the green. Make 20 rows.

ROW 1

From 10 of the rows, sew 1 – 2½" × 4½" blue rectangle to each end.

+ [blurred squares row   ] +   Row 1

ROW 2

From the remaining 10 rows, sew 1 – 1½" × 4½" blue rectangle to one
end and 1 – 3½" × 4½" blue rectangle to the other end.

+ [blurred squares row   ] +   Row 2

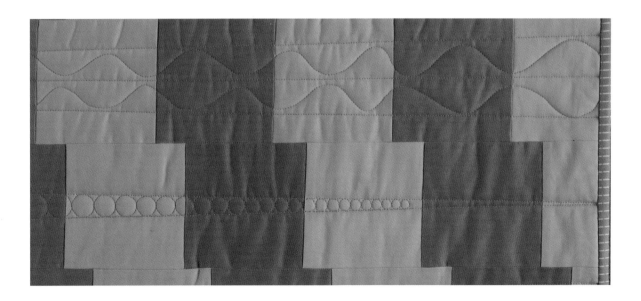

ASSEMBLY

The quilt top is assembled by alternating Rows 1 and 2. Row 2 alternates — half have the 1½" rectangle on the left and the 3½" rectangle on the right; the rest are flipped.

Referring to the diagram, sew Row 1 to Row 2 with the 1½" rectangle on the left side. Then sew the next Row 1 to Row 2 with the 3½" on the left. Make 5 panels (each panel is these 4 rows).

Sew the 5 panels together — make sure Row 1 is always on the top.

Assembly Diagram

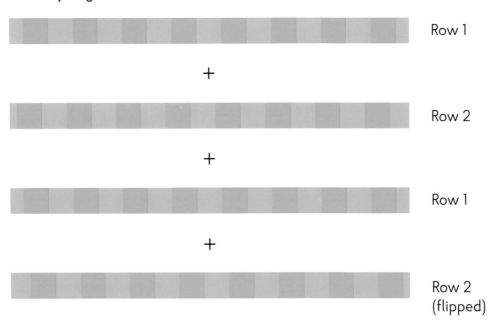

Row 1

+

Row 2

+

Row 1

+

Row 2
(flipped)

FINISHING

BACKING

Piece the backing fabric together to measure 72" × 88".

QUILTING

The quilting is done in wedges: they follow the width of the quilt in each horizontal row to accent the illusion that the rows are narrower on one end than the other. One row is filled with circles and the next row is filled with wavy lines. These alternate down the entire quilt.

BINDING

Make about 308" of binding, using the blue
2½" × width of fabric strips. Bind.

PENNY LAYMAN

Penny is an accomplished paper piecer who designs and teaches (she taught at QuiltCon 2013). Her work has been published in a variety of magazines and books, in addition to her blog. She designs and sells original patterns for paper piecing pattern shop and blog Sew-Ichigo (**sew-ichigo.blogspot.com**). Sewing has been Penny's passion for years. She loves to inspire and teach others, guiding them along their creative journey with joy and lots of laughter. Penny blogs at **sewtakeahike.typepad.com**. She is a member of the Fort Collins Modern Quilt Guild.

OLD DUTCH

MADE AND QUILTED BY MELISSA CORRY

48" × 48" | BLOCK: 12" × 12"

> "On our last family trip, I found myself looking out the window at fields of enormous windmills. If I stared for a few minutes, the angled blades started to look as if they were moving towards me. It was such a fun little optical trick — I found myself shaking my head to clear my vision. That windmill trick was the inspiration for my design, trying to recreate that illusion of the 'windmills' lifting right out of the quilt. Even now, I find myself shaking my head once again after staring at the quilt too long."

FABRIC/ SUPPLIES

- ¼ yard light gray solid
- ¼ yard dark gray solid
- 1 fat eighth each of 5 coordinated solids for windmills
- 1 fat quarter each of 2 coordinated solids for outer triangles
- 2 yards cream for block backgrounds
- 1½ yards print and ⅔ yard contrasting print for pieced backing
- ½ yard black for binding

CUTTING

BLOCKS

- From dark gray, cut 16 – 4" × 4" squares.
- From light gray, cut 16 – 4" × 4" squares.
- From each of 5 coordinated solids, cut 2 – 7¼" × 7¼" squares.
- From each of 2 coordinated solids, cut 3 – 7¼" × 7¼" squares.
- From cream, cut:
  - 32 – 4" × 4" squares
  - 64 – 3⅞" × 3⅞" squares
  - 64 – 3½" × 3½" squares

BACKING

- From backing print, cut 1 – 28" × 54" rectangle and 1 – 14" × 54" rectangle.
- From contrasting print, cut 2 – 12" × width of fabric rectangles.

BINDING

- From black, cut 6 – 2½" × 42" strips.

PIECING

HALF-SQUARE TRIANGLE UNITS

Make 32 – 3½" × 3½" squares light gray/cream and 32 – 3½" × 3½" squares dark gray/cream units.

Draw a diagonal line on the back of the 4" × 4" light and dark gray squares. Place them right sides together with 32 cream squares. Sew ¼" away from either side of the marked line. Cut apart along the marked line. Press both pieces toward the gray. Trim to 3½" × 3½".

Make 32 dark gray and 32 light gray.
3½" × 3½" unfinished.

 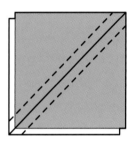 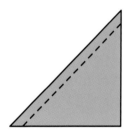 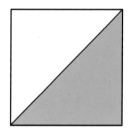

FLYING GEESE UNITS

Make 16 sets of 4 – 3½" × 6½" units – 64 total.

Place 2 – 3⅞" × 3⅞" cream squares on 1 – 7¼" × 7¼" colored square with right sides together. Draw a diagonal line from the top left to the bottom right corner. Sew ¼" away from either side of the drawn line. Cut apart along the marked line. Press the seams toward the cream squares.

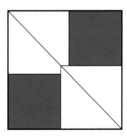 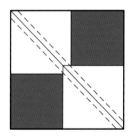 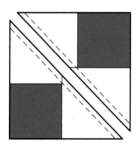

Place a 3⅞" cream square onto each of the 2 pieced units with right sides together. Draw a diagonal line from the top left to the bottom right corner. Sew ¼" away from either side of the drawn line. Cut apart along the marked line. Press the seams toward the cream squares.

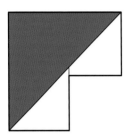 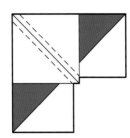 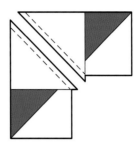

Trim the excess points from the sides and top of each of the 4 units.

Make 16 sets total (4 units per set)
3½" × 6½" unfinished.

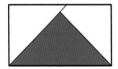  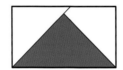 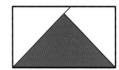

QUARTER UNITS

Make 64 – 6½" × 6½" quarter units.

Note: Color placement is very important for the success of this quilt top. For each set of 4 flying geese, match 2 dark gray half-square triangles and 2 light gray half-square triangles to create 4 quarter units.

Lay out 1 flying geese unit, 1 half-square triangle unit, and 1 – 3½" × 3½" cream square. Sew the cream square and half-square triangle unit together. Sew to the flying geese unit. Press the seams open.

Make 64 quarter units.
6½" × 6½" unfinished.

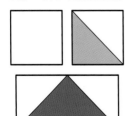 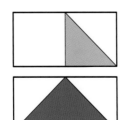 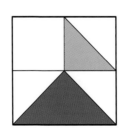

BLOCK ASSEMBLY

Make 16 – 12½" × 12½" blocks.

On a design wall or bed, lay out 4 quarter units, being careful with color placement so the 9 pinwheels in the center of the quilt show (see Assembly Diagram). Sew the units together in 2 rows. Press the seams open. Sew the rows together. Press the seams open.

Make 16.
12½" × 12½" unfinished.

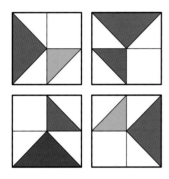
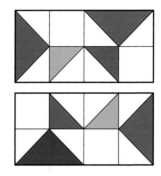
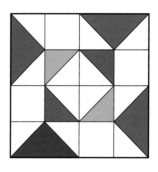

ASSEMBLY

Lay out the blocks in 4 rows of 4 blocks each. Sew the blocks together into 4 rows. Sew the rows together. Press all seams open.

Assembly Diagram

FINISHING

BACKING

Using a ½" seam allowance, sew the 2 contrasting print rectangles together into 1 long strip. Press the seams to the side. Sew the trimmed contrasting strip in between the 2 main print strips to create the quilt backing. Trim to 54" × 54".

Backing Assembly

QUILTING

Quilt in a large spiral. This adds to the optical illusion as your eye follows the spiral out from the center.

BINDING

Using the 6 black binding strips, make about 240" of binding. Bind. ✖

MELISSA CORRY

Melissa started quilting about 10 years ago. However, in the last few years, her hobby has turned into a passion. Starting a blog to share that passion seemed the natural thing to do. Her blog led to creating her own designs, which she shares as tutorials, published works and even her own patterns. Melissa loves designing and finds inspiration everywhere. Melissa, her husband, and their five little children live in Cedar City, Utah. To follow her daily quilting adventures, check out her blog: Happy Quilting (**www.happyquiltingmelissa.com**).

Thank you to Oakshott Cottons for providing the beautiful fabrics for this quilt. Thank you to Christine Powell for being a constant sounding board on all things quilty. And thank you to Barbara Corry for hand binding this quilt and always being there.

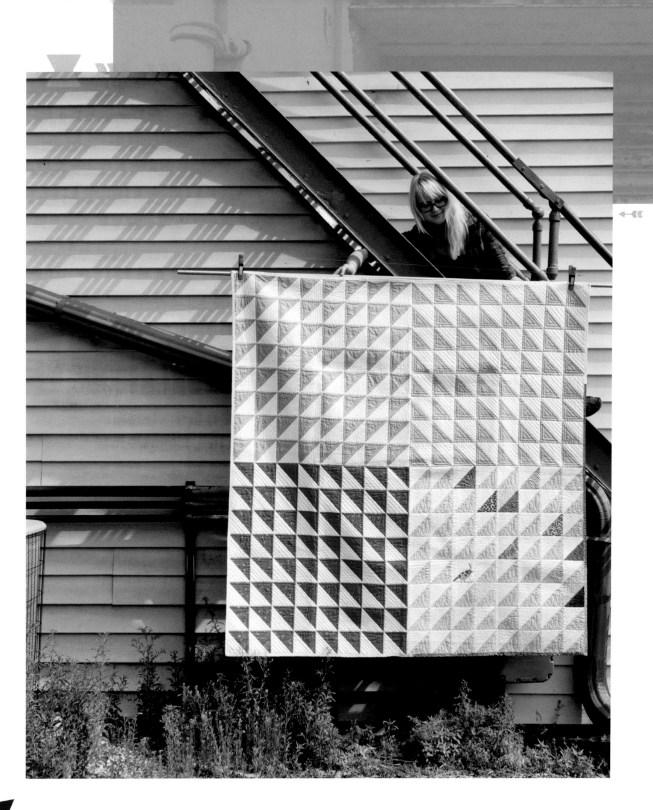

CURVILINEAR

MADE AND QUILTED BY KATIE LARSON

80" × 80" | BLOCK: 20" × 20"

" *I started by researching the most basic optical illusions. I was drawn towards repeating/reflecting patterns and played around with high contrasting colors with pops of color. The quilt is made of varying triangles, but appears to have curves. Depending on where your eyes focus, different designs and depths come into the foreground."*

FABRIC/ SUPPLIES

- 1¾ yards pink for blocks and binding
- 3 yards gray
- 4 yards light blue
- 5 yards for backing
- Water-soluble pen
- Light tape

CUTTING

- Fold each fabric in half, matching selvage to selvage. Cut the rectangles and squares in the sizes listed below. Cut each pair once diagonally from corner to corner to make 2 mirror image triangles.

Note: To stay organized, mark each piece (with a water-soluble pen or light tape) as you cut with the appropriate letter.

- From the light blue, cut:
  - 8 – 8⅝" × 8⅝" squares (A)
  - 16 – 6⅜" × 8⅞" rectangles (B1, B2)
  - 8 – 6½" × 6½" squares (C)
  - 16 – 5" × 9" rectangles (D1, D2)
  - 16 – 5⅛" × 6⅝" rectangles (E1, E2)
  - 16 – 2¾" × 9⅞" rectangles (F1, F2)
  - 16 – 2¾" × 7¼" rectangles (G1, G2)
  - 8 – 5¼" × 5¼" squares (H)
  - 16 – 2⅞" × 5⅝" rectangles (i1, i2)
  - 8 – 3" × 3" squares (J)

- From the gray, cut:
  - 8 – 8⅝" × 8⅝" squares (A)
  - 16 – 6⅜" × 8⅞" rectangles (B1, B2)
  - 16 – 5⅛" × 6⅝" rectangles (E1, E2)
  - 16 – 2¾" × 9⅞" rectangles (F1, F2)
  - 16 – 2¾" × 7¼" rectangles (G1, G2)
  - 8 – 5¼" × 5¼" squares (H)
  - 16 – 2⅞" × 5⅝" rectangles (i1, i2)
  - 8 – 3" × 3" squares (J)

- From the pink, cut:
  - 8 – 6½" × 6½" squares (C)
  - 16 – 5" × 9" rectangles (D1, D2)
  - 8 – 2½" × width of fabric strips for the binding

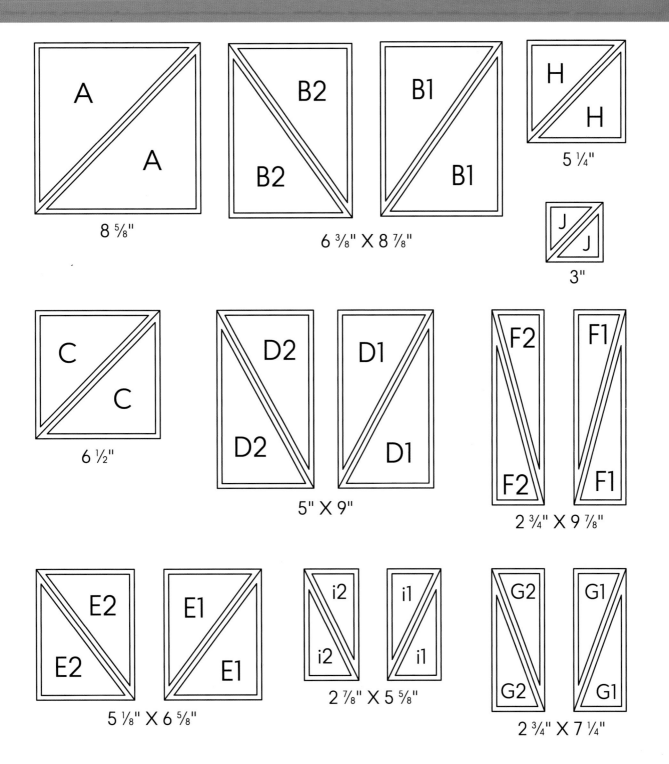

A

A

8 ⅝"

B2

B2

B1

B1

6 ⅜" X 8 ⅞"

H

H

5 ¼"

J

J

3"

C

C

6 ½"

D2

D2

D1

D1

5" X 9"

F2

F2

F1

F1

2 ¾" X 9 ⅞"

E2

E2

E1

E1

5 ⅛" X 6 ⅝"

i2

i2

i1

i1

2 ⅞" X 5 ⅝"

G2

G2

G1

G1

2 ¾" X 7 ¼"

PIECING

Lay out all the half-rectangle triangle pairs: B1&2, D1&2, E1&2, F1&2, G1&2 and i1&2. Sew the pairs together to make 8 each. Press seams open.

Note: For accuracy when sewing, mark a ¼" seam allowance on each half-rectangle triangle listed above.

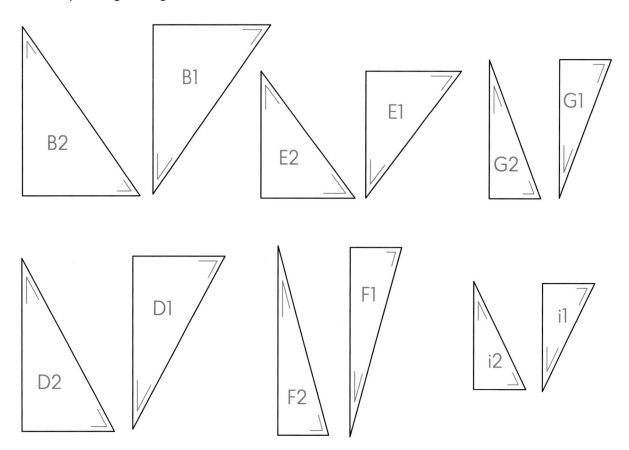

Lay out the pieces for the quarter block according to the diagram (right). Sew together in rows and join the rows. Press seams open. Make 16 quarter blocks.

Sew into rows:

A to B1 to D1 to F1

B2 to C to E1 to G1

D2 to E2 to H to i1

F2 to G2 to i2 to J

Sew the rows together. Press the seams open.

Join 4 quarter blocks together making sure a small, light square is formed in the center of the block. See Assembly Diagram on page 48.

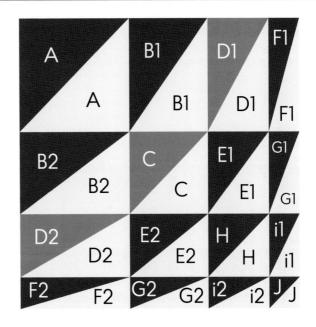

ASSEMBLING

Lay out the blocks according to the Assembly Diagram. Sew the blocks together. Press the seams open. Join the 4 blocks to complete the top.

Assembly Diagram

FINISHING

BACKING

Piece the backing fabric together to measure 88" × 88".

QUILTING

Curvilinear quilting was stitched in the ditch.

BINDING

Make about 320" of binding using the pink 2½" × width of fabric strips. Bind. ✖

Katie made this version also, using only one block of this pattern.

KATIE LARSON

My mother taught me to sew at a young age, and with the help of my mom, I made my first quilt in the eighth grade. I sewed off and on throughout the years, and started quilting again after joining the Kansas City Modern Quilt Guild. I blog occasionally at **thecraftingshell.blogspot.com**.

AURA

MADE AND QUILTED BY JAIME DAVID

60" × 70" | BLOCK: 18" × 24"

"This quilt was inspired by Josef Alber's book, The Interaction of Color. I discovered an optical illusion image online that used color to create a glowing effect, and this served as the basis of my quilt design. The success of this quilt is all about color selection and placement. Unlike painting, with fabrics you cannot mix colors to create a new color, but by using color placement, our eyes perceive a blended color. In this quilt, I varied the shade and tones of analogous color schemes and arranged them in value order. Some of the colors might even clash, but the perceived blending creates an effect of depth in the quilt blocks. There is a secondary illusion created by using rectilinear shapes to create the look of an oval shape."

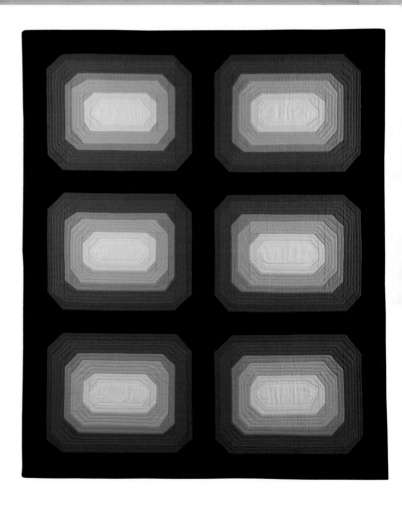

FABRIC/ SUPPLIES

- 7 step gradation:
  - ⅓ yard fabric 1 (lightest for block center)
  - ½ yard fabric 2
  - ¾ yard fabric 3
  - ½ yard fabric 4
  - 1 yard fabric 5
  - ¾ yard fabric 6 (darkest)
  - 2½ yards fabric 7 for sashing and binding
- 4 yards for backing

CUTTING

BLOCKS

- From fabric 1, cut:
  - 6 – 4½" × 10½" rectangles

- From fabric 2, cut:
  - 12 – 1½" × 10½" strips
  - 12 – 1½" × 6½" strips
  - 24 – 2" × 2" squares

- From fabric 3, cut:
  - 12 – 2½" × 12½" strips
  - 12 – 2½" × 10½" strips
  - 24 – 2½" × 2½" squares

- From fabric 4, cut:
  - 12 – 1½" × 16½" strips
  - 12 – 1½" × 12½" strips
  - 24 – 3" × 3" squares

- From fabric 5, cut:
  - 12 – 2½" × 18½" strips
  - 12 – 2½" × 16½" strips
  - 24 – 3" × 3" squares

- From fabric 6, cut:
  - 12 – 1½" × 22½" strips
  - 12 – 1½" × 18½" strips
  - 24 – 3" × 3" squares

BLOCKS AND SASHING

- From fabric 7, cut:
  - 8 – 4" × 24½" strips
  - 5 – 4" × width of fabric strips
  - 24 – 3" × 3" squares

BINDING

- From fabric 7, cut 7 strips 2½" × width of fabric.

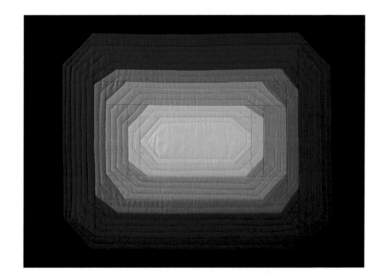

PIECING

Sew a fabric 1 – 4½" × 10½" rectangle to a fabric 2 – 2" × 2" square diagonally on each of the 4 corners. Press back. Trim to 4½" × 10½".

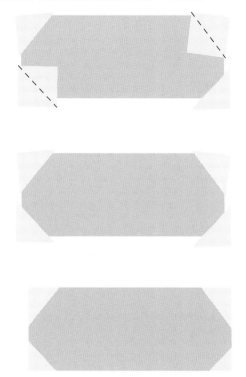

Note: Press each square in half on the diagonal. Use the pressed line as a stitching guide for sewing on the corners.

Sew the 1½" × 10½" fabric 2 strips to the top and bottom of the center unit. Press toward fabric 2. Stitch the 1½" × 6½" strips to the sides. Press.

Repeat this process for each color ring, trimming the central block to size as you go:

Fabric 3: trim center block to 6½" × 12½".

Fabric 4: 10½" × 12½"

Fabric 5: 12½" × 18½"

Fabric 6: 16½" × 22½"

Fabric 7: 18½" × 24½"

Make 6 – 18½" × 24½" blocks.

ASSEMBLY

Lay out the 6 blocks in 2 columns of 3 blocks each. Sew a sashing strip to the top and bottom of each block as shown in the Assembly Diagram. Press toward the sashing.

Sew the 4 – 4" × width of fabric strips together into a long strip. Measure the columns through the center from top to bottom, and cut the strip into 3 strips this length. Sew a strip inbetween the columns and to each side of the top. Press toward the sashing.

Assembly Diagram

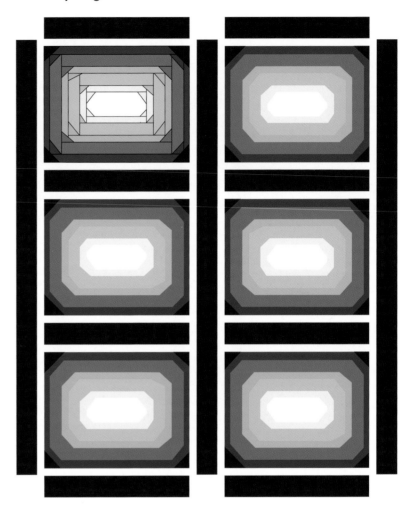

FINISHING

BACKING

Piece the backing fabric into a 68" × 78" rectangle.

QUILTING

Aura was quilted on a domestic machine with radiating straight lines around the shape of the block center. Three color values of thread further emphasize the color change.

BINDING

Join the 2½" strips together to make about 280" of binding. Bind. ✖

Jaime made this version also, in an alternate colorway.

JAIME DAVID

Jaime David has a bachelor's degree in interior architecture and is currently pursuing a masters of fine art in textiles at the University of Kansas. She was a founding member of the Kansas City Modern Quilt Guild. An avid Bernina enthusiast, she has been selling Bernina machines since 2008. Jaime works in Kansas City as a textiles artist and has made it her mission to share the joy of sewing with others by teaching workshops and classes.

Acknowledgments: Robert Kauffman, Kona cotton fabric, Bernina sewing machines, the University of Kansas. Special thanks to my husband, Trey Hock, who never doubts me when I fill life's plate too full.

SURF'S UP!

MADE AND QUILTED BY KAREN HANSEN

51" × 67" | BLOCK: 12" × 12"

" *Having recently completed a bulls-eye quilt for a charity auction, I had some extra blocks left over. Wondering how they would look on point, I began playing with them on my design wall. I realized when the rows are staggered slightly, it creates a pulsating effect, giving the illusion of waves. Thus, Surf's Up! was born, with blue waves rolling into shore, breaking on the sand in the sunlight.*"

FABRIC/ SUPPLIES

* 1 5/8 yards white for blocks

* 2 yards gray for blocks and binding

* 7/8 yard each of dark solid orange and dark solid turquoise for large circles

* 1/3 yard each of 4 orange prints for small circles

* 1/3 yard each of 4 turquoise prints for small circles

* 2 3/4 yards for backing

* Spray starch

* Compass

CUTTING

* From the white and gray, cut 12 – 12 1/2" × 12 1/2" squares each.

* Use the templates on page 65 or use a compass to draw the circle on the backside of the fabric.

* From the solid orange and turquoise, cut 12 – 8 1/2" circles each. Since this is raw edge appliqué, no seam allowance needs to be added.

* From the orange and turquoise prints, cut 12 – 5 1/2" circles each.

* From the gray, cut 7 - 2 1/2" × width of fabric strips for the binding.

Note: Spray the orange and turquoise fabric with starch before cutting the circles. This adds stability when sewing the appliqué.

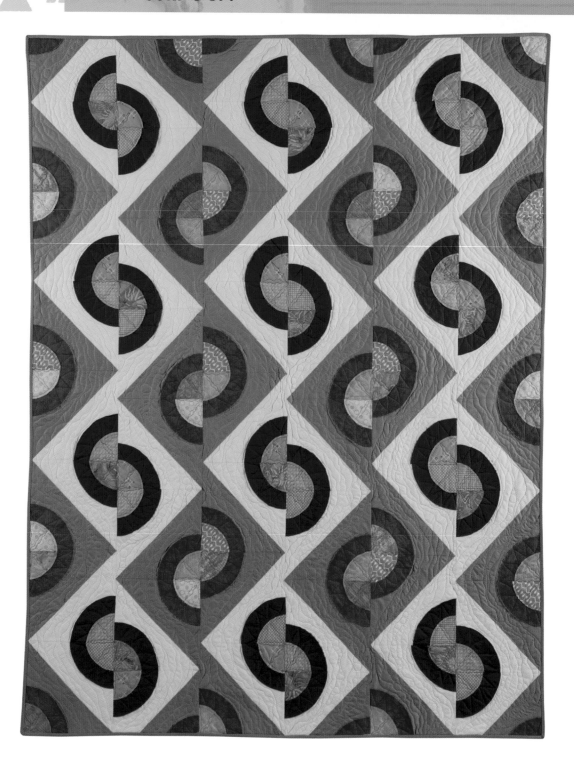

APPLIQUÉ

Fold and finger press each background square and circle in half and half again to find the center.

Center the large turquoise circles on the white background squares by lining up the fold lines. Pin each circle in place and stitch ¼" away from the outer edge of the circle. Repeat with the large orange circles on the gray background. Make 12 of each colorway.

On the back of the block, carefully pull the background fabric away from the solid circle and trim out the background fabric, ¼" inside the stitching line.

Repeat the same steps for the small circles, placing orange on orange and turquoise on turquoise. Make 12 blocks of each colorway.

BLOCKS

Cut each block in half on the diagonal twice to make 4 quarter-square triangles. Make 48 orange quarter-squares and 48 turquoise quarter-squares.

Set aside 12 orange quarter-squares of various prints. These will be placed at the top and bottom of the orange rows.

On your design wall, randomly pair orange triangles together to make 18 half-square triangles. Repeat with the turquoise quarter-squares to make 24 half-square triangles. Sew the quarters together and press toward one side.

ASSEMBLY

Sew the triangles together by vertical rows, top to bottom, matching the points, being careful not to stretch the bias. Press toward the darker fabric.

Pin together rows 1 to 2, 3 to 4, and 5 to 6, carefully matching the placement (follow the diagram).

Note: It is easy to misalign the rows at this point, so recheck the diagram against your placement before joining the rows. Sew the rows together.

Pin row 2 to row 3, carefully matching the placement. Sew the rows together and press toward the side, being careful not to stretch the bias edge. Repeat to sew row 4 to row 5.

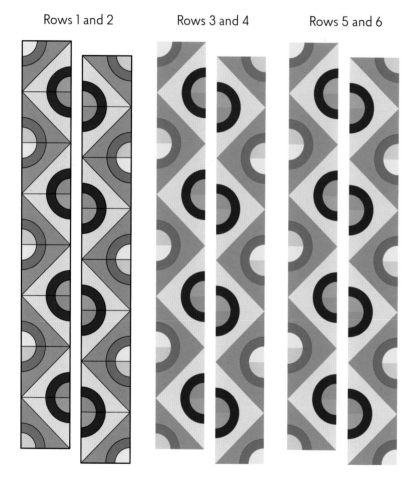

Rows 1 and 2   Rows 3 and 4   Rows 5 and 6

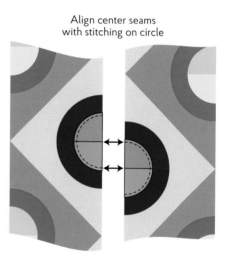

Align center seams with stitching on circle

With a ruler and rotary cutter, square up and trim excess fabric off the top and bottom of the quilt.

Assembly Diagram

Rows 1 and 2   Rows 3 and 4   Rows 5 and 6

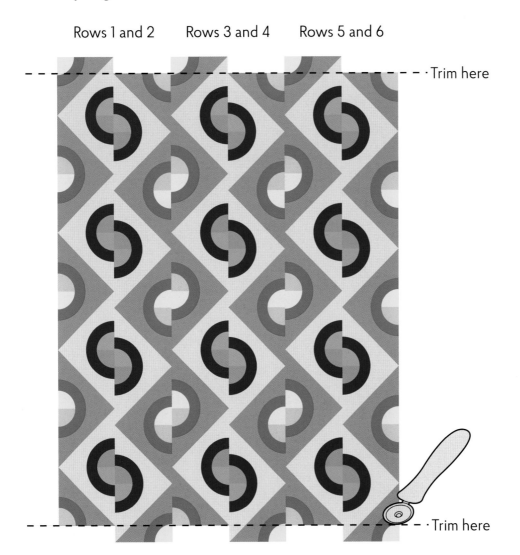

····Trim here

····Trim here

Karen used some leftover circles on her quilt back.

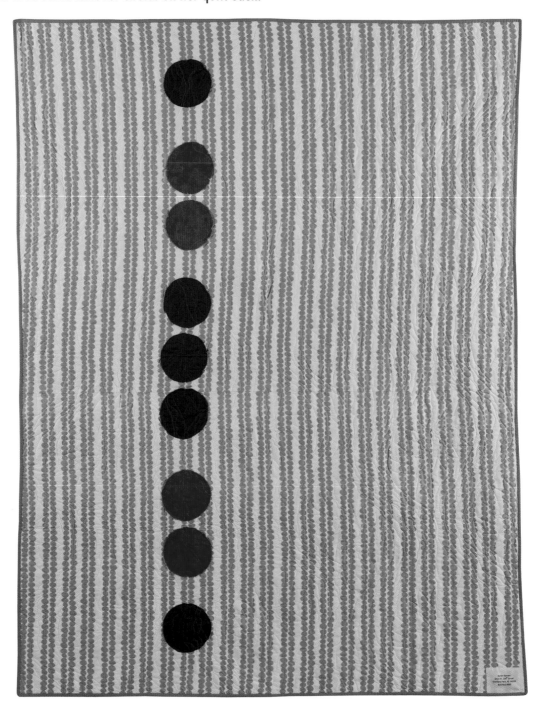

FINISHING

BACKING

Piece the backing fabric together to measure 59" × 75".

QUILTING

Surf's Up! was quilted on a domestic sewing machine. The background blocks were quilted from top to bottom in wavy lines to resemble waves (pattern on page 64). Bubbles were quilted in various channels. The centers of the blocks are a simple flower/seaweed design, and the solid circles are quilted with a zigzag.

BINDING

Make about 260" of binding using the gray 2½" × width of fabric strips. Bind. ✖

KAREN HANSEN

Karen Hansen started quilting in 2000, quickly transitioning from traditional patterns to designing her own modern and art quilts. She has taught workshops at local shops and guilds, and her work has been published in various books and magazines. Her quilts have won prizes in local shows and have been juried into the AQS show in Paducah, Kentucky. Her commissioned works are displayed in churches and individuals' homes.

Karen lives in Overland Park, Kansas, with her husband and three cats. She is a member of Blue Valley Quilt Guild, Kaw Valley Quilt Guild, Kansas City Modern Guild and Studio Art Quilt Associates.

Thanks to my husband, Frank, for his patience putting up with late dinners and a messy house, and for his software assistance in illustrating the pattern. Thanks also to Deb and Jenifer for their support and assistance.

Quilting designs

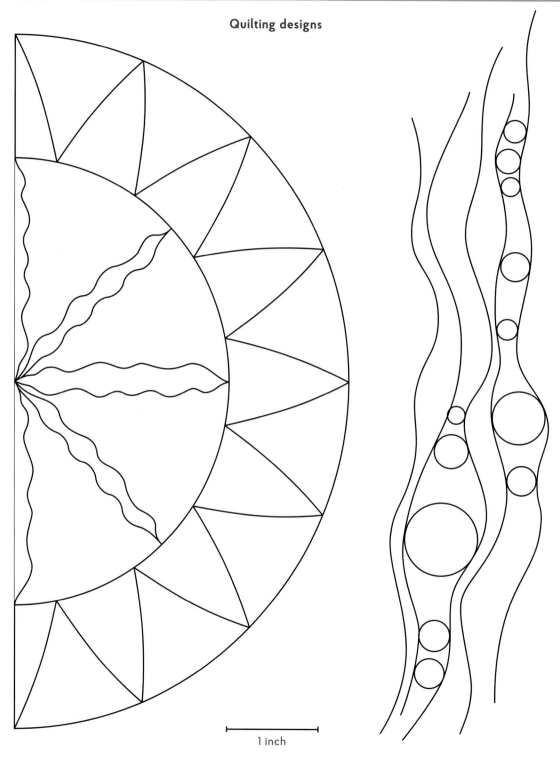

1 inch

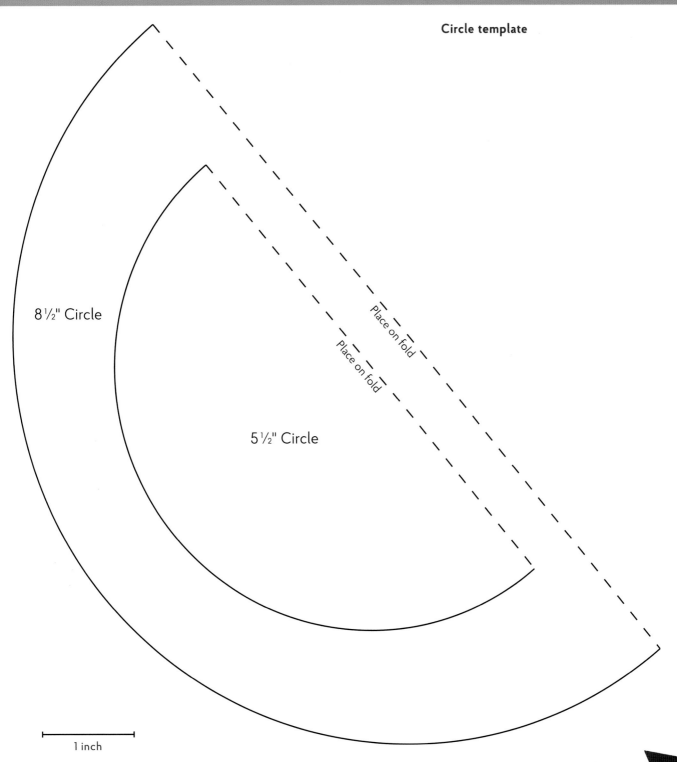

Circle template

8 ½" Circle

5 ½" Circle

Place on fold

Place on fold

1 inch

3-D DIAMONDS

MADE BY JENIFER DICK | QUILTED BY TIA CURTIS
61" × 46" | BLOCK: 4" × 4"

> *3-D Diamonds is influenced by Victor Vasarely, widely regarded as the father of op art. His 1967 poster, London Art Gallery, is a series of black and gray squares that gradually shift from squares to diamonds. To me, it looked like the traditional Tumbling block. Blending his style with a traditional quilt block made this unexpected 3-D rendition of an optical illusion quilt!"*

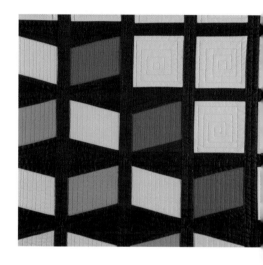

FABRIC/ SUPPLIES

- 3 yards dark gray (includes sashing and binding)
- ¼ yard medium gray
- ¼ yard light gray
- ½ yard light blue
- ½ yard lighter blue
- ½ yard lightest blue
- ¼ yard red
- ¼ yard gold
- ¼ yard orange
- 5" square creamy yellow
- ½ yard bright yellow
- 3 yards light gray or other light color for backing
- Your favorite paper piecing papers and supplies

CUTTING

BLOCKS

- From medium gray, cut 4 – 4½" squares.

  - From light gray, cut 8 – 4½" squares.

  - From light blue, cut 24 – 4½" squares.

  - From lighter blue, cut 16 – 4½" squares.

  - From lightest blue, cut 24 – 4½" squares.

PAPER-PIECED BLOCKS*

* From red, cut 7 – 5" squares.
* From orange, cut 5 – 5" squares.
* From gold, cut 3 – 5" squares.
* From creamy yellow, cut 1 – 5" square.
* From bright yellow, cut 16 – 5" squares.
* From the dark gray, cut 64 – 2½" × 5½" rectangles for paper-pieced blocks.

SASHING

* From the dark gray, cut:
  1. 96 – 1½" × 4½" strips for sashing
  1. 13 – 1½" × 44½" strips for sashing
  1. 2 – 1½" × 61½" strips for sashing

BINDING

* From the dark gray, cut 4 – 2½" × width of fabric strips for binding.

Note: If you are a frugal paper-piecer, cut these fabrics smaller. If you are a generous paper-piecer, cut them larger. Make a sample block first to find out what sizes you are comfortable with.

PAPER PIECING

Each paper-pieced block consists of the main body color and 2 dark gray triangles.

Note: The bright yellow blocks are configured differently from the rest. Use the PP1 template (page 69) to make them and the PP2 template (page 70) for the remaining blocks. Use 1 – 5" square and 2 – 2½" × 5½" rectangles per block and paper piece the following. After piecing, trim each to 4½".

Using the PP1 template, make 16 Block A:

* 16 bright yellow/gray blocks

Using the PP2 template (page 70), make 16 Block B:

* 7 red/gray blocks
* 5 orange/gray blocks
* 3 gold/gray blocks
* 1 creamy yellow/gray block

Make 16 Block A in bright yellow.

Make 16 Block B in red, orange, gold and creamy yellow.

ASSEMBLY

Referring to the Assembly Diagram, lay out the blocks on your design wall or the floor. Be very careful to place the blue background blocks properly. Since there is very little difference in color, it's easy to mix them up. Place the darkest blues at the top, and the lightest at the bottom.

Sew 8 – 1½" × 4½" sashing strips in between the blocks in columns. Join the columns with 11 – 41½" sashing strips. Sew the remaining 2 – 41½" strips to the sides. Sew 2 – 1½" × 61½" strips to the top and bottom to finish.

PP1 template

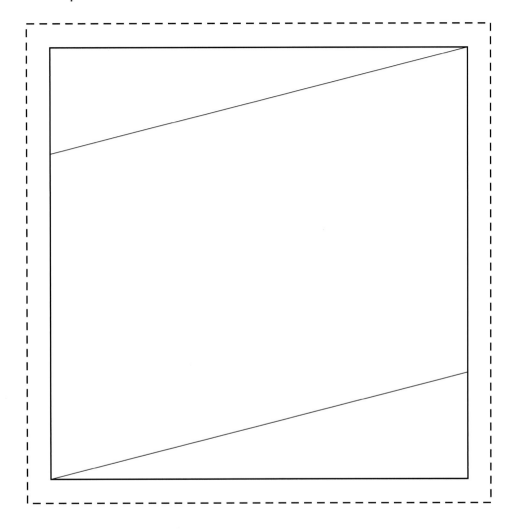

1 inch

PP2 template

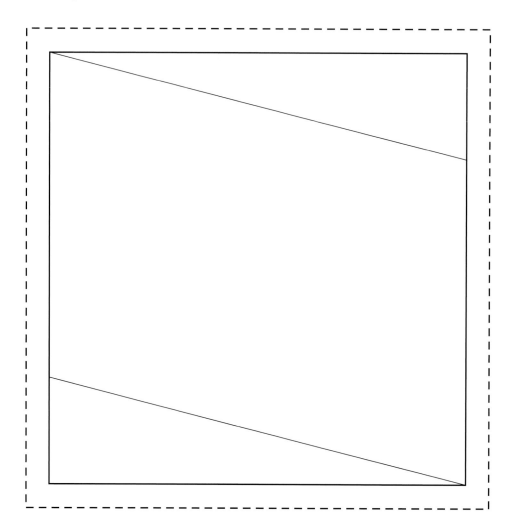

1 inch

Assembly Diagram

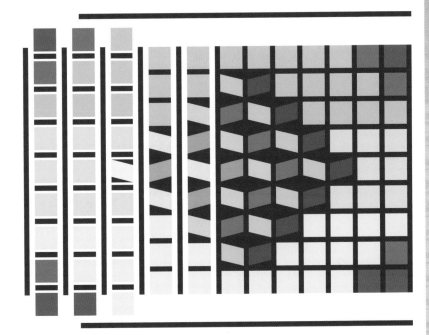

FINISHING

BACKING

Piece the backing fabric together to measure 54" × 69".

QUILTING

To accentuate the 3-D effect, quilt the pieced blocks with a combination of diamonds in the gray areas, and straight vertical lines in the colored areas. Quilt each blue and gray square with continuous-line squares in each. The sashing is quilted with triple straight lines.

BINDING

Make about 135" of binding, using the dark gray 2½" × width of fabric strips. Bind. ✻

JENIFER DICK

Jenifer began quilting in 1993, when on a whim, she signed up for a beginning quiltmaking class. From that first stitch she was hooked. In 2005, she wrote her first book and has been talking to guilds and teaching appliqué to quiltmakers ever since. She is the author of five quilt books on topics from traditional to modern, and her work has been published in many other books and magazines. Jenifer lives in Harrisonville, Missouri, with her husband and three teenagers. Follow her on her blog, 42 Quilts, at **42quilts.com**.

TANGERINE TUMBLER

MADE AND QUILTED BY MARY KAY FOSNACHT

40" × 40"

The Tumbler block has been around for a long time, but when done in shades of light, medium and dark, it takes on a dimensional, 'building-type' feel. I think the diamond shape adds dimension and, when given a pop of color, brings the whole quilt to life. It is a simple quilt to construct with big impact. You can always add more background or another set of tumblers to make it bigger. You can change the orange to hot pink or even a cool blue to simulate the reflection of the sky. Choose your favorite pop of color to make it your own!"

FABRIC/ SUPPLIES

- ⅓ yard orange solid
- ⅓ yard light gray
- 1 yard dark gray for blocks and binding
- ½ yard black
- 1 yard white
- 2 yards for backing
- ¼ yard orange for flange (optional)
- Template plastic or freezer paper to make templates
- Spray starch
- Water soluble gluestick (optional)

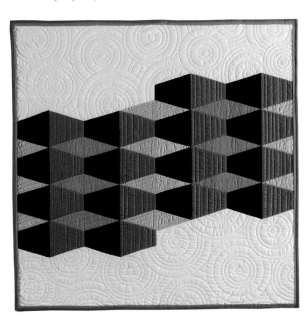

CUTTING

Using the templates on page 78, make 1 tumbler template and 1 half-diamond template from the template plastic or freezer paper.

+ From the dark gray, black **and** white, cut 2 – 5 ½" × width of fabric strips. Using the tumbler template, subcut into 16 tumbler shapes **of each color.**

+ From the light gray, cut 2 – 5 ½" × width of fabric strips. Using the half-diamond template, subcut into 14 half-diamond shapes.

+ From the orange, cut 2 – 5 ½" × width of fabric strips. Using the half-diamond template, subcut into 12 half-diamond shapes.

+ From the white, cut:

  ▪ 2 – 5 ½" × 20 ½" strips for the background

  ▪ 2 – 11 ½" × 20 ½" rectangles for the background

+ From the dark gray, cut 5 – 2 ½" × width of fabric strips for the binding.

+ From the orange, cut 5 – 1 ¼" × width of fabric strips for the flange (optional).

PIECING

The top center is sewn together in 8 columns.

To make column 1: lay out 2 white tumbler shapes, 4 black tumbler shapes and 3 light gray half-diamond shapes. Sew together alternating the black and light gray. Sew the 2 whites to the ends. Sew with the diamond point on top when possible.

Note: Offset the tumblers and diamond shapes by ¼" so the column will line up straight after sewing.

To make columns 2 and 6: Using the same direction as above, sew 4 dark gray tumbler shapes alternating with 3 orange half-diamond shapes. Sew the 2 white tumbler shapes to the ends.

To make columns 3 and 7: Sew 4 black tumbler shapes alternating with 3 orange half-diamond shapes. Sew the 2 white tumbler shapes to the ends.

To make column 4: Sew 4 dark gray tumbler shapes alternating with 4 light gray half-diamond shapes. Sew the 2 white tumbler shapes to the ends.

To make column 5: Sew 4 black tumbler shapes alternating with 4 light gray half-diamond shapes. Sew the 2 white tumbler shapes to the ends.

To make column 8: Sew 4 dark gray tumbler shapes alternating with 3 light gray half-diamond shapes. Sew the 2 white tumbler shapes to the ends.

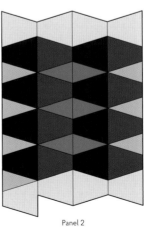

Column 1 Column 2 Column 3 Column 4

Column 5 Column 6 Column 7 Column 8

Panel 1

Panel 2

Join columns 1-4 and 5-8 together to make 2 panels. Press the seams toward one side. Trim the top and bottom 2" from the "peak" of the black/gray tumblers, keeping the cut perpendicular to the edges and vertical seams.

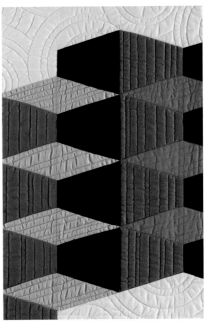

Column 1   Column 2   Column 3   Column 4

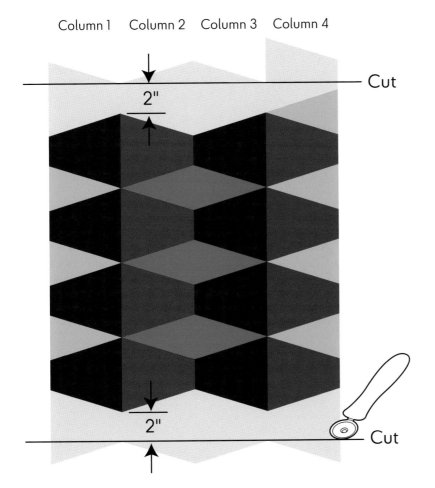

— Cut

2"

2"

Cut

ASSEMBLY

Sew 1 of the 5½" × 20½" strips to the bottom of Panel 1. Sew the other strip to the top of Panel 2.

Sew 1 of the 11½" × 20½" strips to the top of Panel 1. Sew the other strip to the bottom of Panel 2.

Sew Panel 1 to Panel 2, matching the seams at the tumbler intersections.

Assembly Diagram

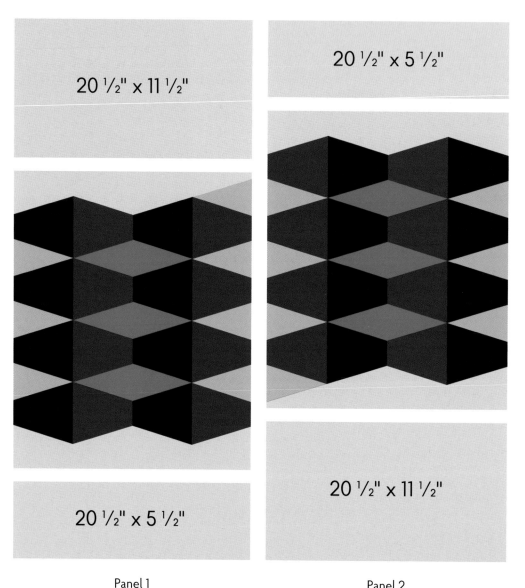

Panel 1

Panel 2

FINISHING

BACKING

Piece the backing fabric into a 48" × 48" square.

QUILTING

Tangerine Tumbler was quilted with vertical lines in the tumbler shapes and horizontal lines in the diamonds. Concentric circles about 8" round overlap in the background to add contrast.

BINDING

Join the binding strips to make about 200" of binding. Bind.

If making the flange, fold the 4 – 1¼" orange strips in half lengthwise with right side out. Press to form a long narrow strip.

Pin or glue using a water-soluble gluestick to the quilt top, aligning the raw edges with the outside edge of the quilt. Fold back the strip at each corner with the fold under the strip to form a 45-degree miter. Trim the excess fabric at the outer edge of the quilt.

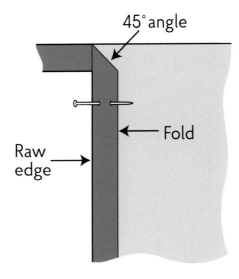

45° angle

Fold

Raw edge

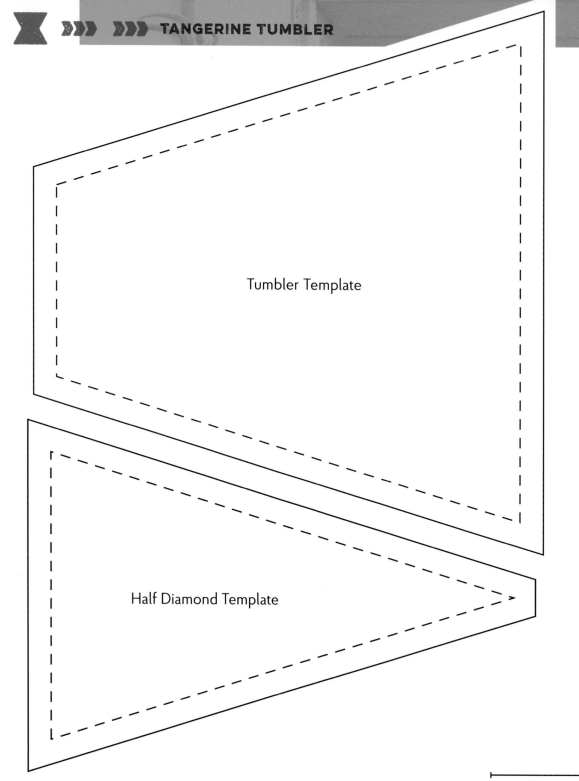

Tumbler Template

Half Diamond Template

1 inch

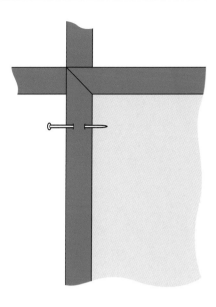

Attach the gray binding on top of the orange as usual. When the binding is folded to the back, the flange will be revealed. ✕

Leftover blocks are used on the back — and for a quilt label.

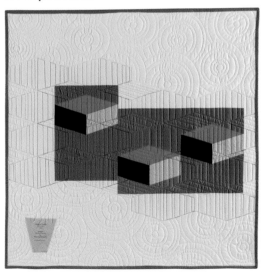

MARY KAY FOSNACHT

Mary Kay was born in Chicago and graduated from Illinois Benedictine University with degrees in music education and sacred music. In the early 1990s, she and her husband and two children moved to Overland Park, Kansas, where they still reside. As she said after the move, "My husband went to work, the kids went to school, and I went to the fabric store!" Thus began her quilting journey.

Mary Kay enjoys the entire process of quiltmaking from conception to adding a label, especially the creative aspect of taking a thought and making it tangible. The modern aesthetic has allowed her to grow her creativity in a new way. In her spare time, she enjoys hiking in the mountains in Colorado, playing piano and photography.

I would like to acknowledge my husband, Fred, for his ever-enthusiastic support of all my sewing endeavors.